IT'S
A
WUDDLEFUL
LIFE

DANNY
BURRIS

It's a Wuddleful Life
Danny Burris

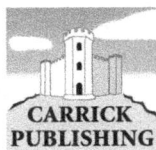

**CARRICK
PUBLISHING**

Copyright Danny Burris 2017
Carrick Publishing
Print Edition 2017
ISBN 13: 978-1-77242-066-1
Cover Design Donna Carrick
Cover Background Photo
© Can Stock Photo / VadimPetrov

Print Edition, License Notes:

The stories included in this collection are light-hearted memories of the author. Please enjoy the humor intended and ignore any errors of memory.

Introduction

Hello, my name is Danny, but a lot of people know me as Willie C. Wuddle.

Why the name Willie C. Wuddle? My better half nicknamed me Wuddle many years ago, and it's short for Cuddle Wuddle. I grew the Willie part on my own. ;).

I hope you like my book, as I've wanted to write it for years. The stories are all true to the best of my memory.

This book does not promote religious beliefs, violence, moral issues, politics, or bad haircuts.

It doesn't contain high speed car chases, special effects, overpriced celebrities, or lots of hype.

It is just a book meant to be read and not to be taken seriously. If you like the book, smile to yourself or let out a snicker. If you don't like it, I'm sure you've read worse and should go back to reading *Penthouse Letters*.

I hope you like it.

ATF

It was a nice night and we decided to go for a boat trip in the lake after I got off work. The rest of the crew decided to float down from the trailer park and I'd meet them later at the dock.

As I was waiting, Dennis showed up with a new car. It must have been a police car at one point, because the head lights could flash left and right from side to side.

We decided to have some fun. As the boat got closer to shore we put on all our lights yelling, "This is the ATF. Surrender your drugs and alcohol........This is the ATF. Surrender your drugs and alcohol."

The waves were splashing as the boat got closer. After giving them a scare we both jumped out and laughed at the whole thing.

They got the bigger laugh though. They had panicked and tossed our beer into the lake.

DANNY BURRIS

The Bathroom Puffer

Once I was in the hospital and had to share the bathroom with three other people. There always seemed to be someone in the bathroom, so I started going to the public bathroom down the hall in the next section.

Whenever I used it in the morning it was always full of smoke. Coughing and wheezing, I'd do my business, finish the paper work, and be on my way.

After a couple of weeks I figured I'd had enough. I held my poop in for about three days then went to the bathroom fifteen minutes early. When I was done the air was almost blue. I let it set for a few minutes and it really smelled the room up.

After that day I never smelled smoke in the bathroom again. I think the bathroom puffer found another bathroom to use.

I just hope he didn't blow himself up that day.

Beer at the Hockey Game

Once my oldest brother and I went to see a hockey game at the Moncton Coliseum. It was the semifinals for The Calder Cup, if I recall correctly.

They sold beer so I bought a Molson XXX and, being a neat and tidy person when I'm away from home, threw the cover in the garbage. I then went back to my seat. Soon an usher told me I couldn't have open beer in my section. I swigged the refreshing beverage back and everybody was happy.

I went for another and sat in a different section that was empty. The usher told me no open beer, so again I swigged it back. I got another beer and stood drinking it in the main reception area only to find out about the no open beer rule.

I was becoming annoyed by then, and was buying them and drinking them as fast as I could before the usher had a chance to pester me. Somehow I ended up down by the visitors net and really got excited when Moncton started scoring.

I was standing on the seat cheering away and, due to minor intoxication, fell off and landed on top of some girl. My brother grabbed my arm saying "Dan, you see those guys in the red blazers? They're not the Century 21 boys, you know." I was escorted out of the building by security and proceeded to walk home.

The next night I went to work and looked at the TV in the bar. It showed me being escorted out of the building on the news. This got a round of applause from the customers.

Later I found out it was ok to have beer in the Moncton Coliseum as long as you kept the plastic covers on the cups.

Oh well, I never was the brightest bulb in chandelier.

Boating With My Dad

I remember the first time I went boating with my father in Lake Petitcodiac. I had just bought my first Seahawk 340.

We sipped on some brew as I pumped up the boat. (Actually I blew up the boat, but I don't want to sound like a terrorist.) We were out floating in the lake and I kept asking him, "Are you getting wet yet?"

He kept saying, "No."

Finally, for some reason, he fell out of the boat, sitting on the bottom of the lake with just his head above the water.

"I'm wet now," he said, and I knew he was right.

We eventually went home, calling it a day.

Born To Be (Not So) Wild

I once had a Suzuki 185 Enduro bike. It was great for beating traffic and I took it just about everywhere locally. I really loved that little bike.

One very nice day in February I wondered if it would start. It started on the first kick. I sat on the seat and turned the throttle.

Man, it was running nice, so I took it around the block. It felt so good that I got my helmet and proceeded to take it to Riverview to pick up my pay check.

I was riding west along Queen Street with the 4:30 sun directly behind me. I went through a puddle and my brakes froze up. At the corner of Queen and Alma an elderly gent pulled out in front of me causing me to hit him broad side. Over the car I flew, landing flat on my back.

It was sure hard getting back up and pushing the bike off the road. I looked for my right sneaker, but I think it flew over the construction fence at the base of the telephone tower.

The driver felt quite bad about what had happened, so I climbed into his car and we headed for Hugh's Autobody on Pine Glen Road. We got a good estimate. I figured I was in some kind of wrong riding my motorbike in the winter, especially with no insurance, and offered to pay for half of the damage to his car. My half of the bill was a little more than $200.00, but I figured it was cheaper than getting a fine for no insurance.

He dropped me off at the telephone tower and I looked and looked for my lost sneaker. Finally I gave up and starting pushing the bike home.

The fornicating brakes sure worked good now. They were locked up frozen. It was a hard push through the old east end. I bought 3 bottles of Dr McGillicuddy's pain killer from the beverage store and got poopeyed.

The next day I looked at my back in the mirror and saw a massive bruise of over a square foot in size. I never rode a motorbike in the winter again.

DANNY BURRIS

Break In

I remember many moons ago I lived in a basement apartment. I went out and bought a case of beer and a pizza.

When I got home I realized I'd left my keys inside. It was about 3:00 am so I didn't want to wake anybody up. I proceeded to break into my apartment. I jimmied the window open and started to go inside.

I got stuck in the window and couldn't move. I had a case of beer and a 12 inch pizza with me. What a great time to see a police car show up.

As I waved and struggled to get in the window the two officers started laughing. It was then I realized that nobody breaks into a place with pizza and a case of beer. I laughed so hard that I fell into the window.

Mission accomplished.

Bus to the Beer Store

It was a Friday afternoon and I planned to take the bus to the beer store. The bus wasn't on time. I waited over 45 minutes hoping the half hour circuit would hurry up.

Then it hit me, this was Good Friday and the busses weren't running. Since it was a nice day I decided to walk to the beer store.

I was about 4 streets over when I thought it was Good Friday and the beer store was closed.

Oh well, it was not a very beerful day.

DANNY BURRIS

Camping With My Nephew

My nephew and myself decided to go camping once upon a time. I filled the truck up with gas, bought some food and beer, and we were off to Martin's Head.

Martin's Head was a place I had camped at about 25 years before when I was still in high school. It is a body of land you can walk to when the Bay of Fundy tide is out but turns into an island when the tide comes in.

I decided to park the truck at the old lobster wharf and we would walk the rest of the way. After we had the truck stuck up to the axels in sand, I realized the wharf wasn't there anymore.

We dug and dug but we were stuck. A couple of people helped us push, but we had no results. I had the great idea of driving down the side of the sandbar and hoping to gain enough momentum to come back up again, then just keep on moving.

Down the side I drove. I hit the bottom of the sandbar, which was about 6 feet below where I had previously started. The tide was starting to come in and the truck would soon be under about a foot of water in a couple of hours.

The other people went to get a tow truck. We waited and waited. When it was starting to get dark I saw a tow truck coming way off in the distance. The tow truck had come from Sussex, a town about 50 miles away and the owner drove out of his way on faith to help us out.

After much work he got the truck out. The fee was $150.00, but well worth every penny. It was too dark to put up the tent, so my nephew and I decided to head home. We bought a couple of 12 inch Bravo pizzas on the way and watched the Blue Jays game on TV.

The camping trip had cost me $213.00 and we didn't even get to camp out.

Certificates

I remember being three sheets to the wind and trying to impress Mrs, Wuddle. I got to talking martial arts and told her of a few different styles I studied.

She didn't seem to believe me, so I dug into the bottom dresser drawer and pulled out my stack of certificates.

As I was explaining each, I was neatly placing them on a chair. After I finished, I went to sit down and put my butt through each and every one. What a racket and mess it was.

I never bragged about them again.

Change Room

I remember going to one of the local thrift shops a few years back. The store was quiet so I decided to have some fun.

I went into the change room and yelled, "We're out of terlit paper in here."

I think they took me seriously as they seemed quite cranky. I left the store and haven't come back since then.

Maybe someday I will bring a roll of terlit paper with me.

Cleaning the Walls

I was bored at work once and decided to wash the walls. We had just gotten a new brand of cleaner and I figured I'd test it out.

The guy I worked with told me to only put one cupful per bucket. I washed and scrubbed for two days, really doing a nice job. My right hand was starting to turn a faint yellow colour.

I figured this stuff is really great for cleaning the old smoke off the walls.

The job was finally finished and the other guy asked me what happened to all the cleaner. I told him I used it all up. He didn't believe me.

It turned out he'd meant to say to use one capful per bucket instead of one cupful. My chemical burn eventually faded, after a couple of months.

I let somebody else wash the walls next time.

Dancing at The Cosmo

I do not dance as a rule. I just plain am no good at it. One night I was casually sipping a couple of brew. Ok ok, I was guzzling many brew and ended up at The Cosmo Club in Moncton.

I don't know exactly what happened, but I was asked by a fine looking lady to dance. The little head started thinking, and before I knew it we were on the dance floor.

Soon I had become the world's greatest dancer. I went back to the table and discovered my full beer was missing. I got another and took this one to the dance floor with me. There were 4 girls dancing by themselves so I boogied on over to where they were.

At this time I think the little head was starting to get drunk too. We danced away. I looked behind me and, OH My GOD, there were 4 more girls dancing by themselves. It never occurred to me that if you do a 360 degree turn you might see the same 4 people possibly in a different order.

Eventually the inevitable happened. I dropped my beer in the middle of the dance floor. I stuck my finger in the hole to stop it from foaming over and it sprayed everybody. As the doormen were escorting me out the door, I wondered why people love to get sprayed with champagne on TV but not beer in real life.

Day at the Beach

Many moons ago, my brother and I went to Parlee Beach. We loaded our packsacks with a few brew and were hiking along enjoying the sights. We decided to take a break and enjoy a brew so we sat down on the grass up against a fence.

The first beer magically turned into a second beer and soon a portion of a third one. People were walking by staring at us. Some were whispering and others were snickering.

I asked my brother, "What's the matter, haven't these people ever seen anyone drinking beer before?"

It was then we both realized my cut offs were a bit too short. I ended up with a sunburn on somewhere I'll never forget.

Delivering Pizza

I was relaxing and having a few (9) beers one night and it started snowing quite badly. My better half was delivering pizzas and one of her windshield wipers broke. She didn't feel like driving, so I volunteered to work for her, pretending not to be half in the bag.

The car was always getting stuck and the roads were not fit for driving. I watched the snow on the windshield as it slowly became a big snowball going back and forth under the wiper. I kept throwing the snowball away, but it was snowing so hard that it kept building back up.

Then the second wiper broke. I had a delivery on Trider Crescent, but had to park on Henderson St. and walk about a block through hip deep snow. The person was a bit ticked off for waiting so long, but mellowed out when I showed him where I'd walked through the snow.

Finally I got to the last delivery and set off to Bridgedale to deliver it. The snow on Coverdale Road was almost a foot deep, and the car just crawled through the snow.

I had to walk around to the back the building in chest deep snow to be greeted by a cranky customer who figured he'd waited too long. With the last delivery done, we closed up the shop and all went home.

We got over 60 inches of snow that night, setting a record for Moncton.

Driving in the U.S.A.

I remember my first time driving in the USA. I crossed the border and was on my way. I had a long line of cars following me and a few passed me. A couple didn't wave with all their fingers.

I thought to myself, "Self, is life here in the USA really that much faster than in Canada?"

I kept getting passed and some of the people looked real cranky. I almost told them to take off, eh.

I finally found out what I was doing wrong and why the Americans were so cranky. I was driving 30 kph in the 30 mph zone.

At least at 18 mph I didn't get any speeding tickets.

Drowning

Once, while visiting my better half, I started to have a very hard time breathing. I thought it was the 3 cat's boxes starting to get to me, so I went outside for a walk.

It was about 5:30 am, so I was very quiet while walking up and down the street. My breathing kept getting worse.

Finally I couldn't take it anymore and hollered through the back door that I needed an ambulance. The ambulance came and the EMT technicians gave me oxygen, but I still couldn't breathe. They put me in back of the ambulance and away we went.

The few miles from Bristol to the North Carleton Hospital in Bath seemed to take forever. By the time we arrived, I saw a door. I was going to go through it, but a voice told me that if I went through it I would be stuck with my decision for all time.

The EMT technician hollered and told me to hold on, bringing me back to reality. We made it to the hospital. I got a shot of Lasix and soon had to pee quite badly. They were shoving a catheter up the old ying yang and I asked the nurse if it was ok for me to pee.

She said ok, so I let it go. I guess the tube wasn't in quite all the way because it shot out and I sprayed all over the nearby nurses.

I later learned I had pulmonary edema and was drowning from the inside. It was brought on by not taking my 2 cent water pills for a couple of days. I felt like a real jackass for not taking the pills.

Edith Cavell Airport

I used to be fascinated with paper airplanes. I used to love throwing them from the third floor window at Edith Cavell School.

People used to walk by and watch my airplanes sail over the school yard. I had the idea one day of making a 3 foot plane from some craft paper that I "borrowed" from the art room. That sucker really flew good.

It led to another, then another. I pretended the last one had engine trouble and set it on fire before letting it fly.

After I almost set fire to the school, the art teacher didn't like the whole idea and made me clean up the art room after school for a week.

I decided to close the airport.

Escort Service

I once helped the local deputy sheriff out as an escort. An escort just opens and closes the doors of the transport vehicle letting prisoners in or out of it.

We had one prisoner being transferred from the Moncton Detention Center to the Dalhousie Jail and had to pick up an escapee to be returned to Centracare in Campbellton.

The Moncton Detention center was scary, but the Dalhousie Jail, with its reputation as being the toughest jail in New Brunswick, really made me want to never go there to stay for any length of time.

We picked up the escapee and were on our way again. All was going well. When we got to Centracare I helped out and carried in the escapee's suit cases.

The escapee went off to say hi to his friends. The nurse saw me with the suit cases and proceeded to lead me back to my room.

The deputy sheriff thought this was funny and didn't let on that I was his helper at first. We got things all cleared up and headed back to Moncton.

DANNY BURRIS

Field Goal

I remember after work one night my brother and I decided to pedal to Parlee Beach. The new highway made the trip seem a lot shorter and we made it in record time.

We locked our bikes and started walking down the beach. My brother noticed something on the beach and decided to take a run and give it a kick.

He gave quite a kick. He was very surprised when a guy who was half buried in the sand let out a yell and started chasing him.

We ran back to the bikes and headed back home. I'll bet that was the last time my brother ever interrupted a guy and girl on a beach, covered with blankets at 3:30am.

Fight in the Basement

There was a time once when I went to a party and actually had too much to drink. I ended up sleeping on somebody's couch in the basement.

I recall waking up in the middle of the night and looking for the bathroom. As I stumbled around in the dark, somebody grabbed me. I turned and soon was in a head lock.

I then realized I was outnumbered and started swinging away. They had me on the ground and by then it was almost a losing battle. I somehow got free and went upstairs to the bathroom.

The hostess woke up and asked me what was going on and when I told her about the fight I had in the basement she didn't believe me.

I practically crawled into work the next morning on three toes, badly hung over and ruffed up a bit.

Later the hostess went to take her laundry off the basement clothesline only to find it thrown all over the place. She then put two and two together.

I guess that was the toughest load of laundry I ever fought with.

Fire in the Hat

Once, many many moons ago, my brother and myself were making paper airplanes and throwing them out of his bedroom window. I'm not sure whose idea it was, but he lit one on fire and tossed it out.

It sailed along the length of the driveway and landed on top of the drunk guy next door's hat, setting the hat on fire. The guy was looking around, trying to find where the smoke was coming from.

When he realized his hat was burning, was he ever p155ed off and started swearing.

Geez, what a hot head.

Getting Groceries for Grannie

My friend, Arlene, always picked me up on bowling night. One night she had to pick up some groceries for her grandmother, so off we went to Sobey's in Riverview.

Her grandmother wanted a half pound of Mapleleaf bacon. All they had were one pound packages. They did however have half pound packages of bacon with less salt.

Arlene called her grandmother to see if it was ok to get the less-salt bacon. Grannie was 98 years old and a bit hard of hearing, so Arlene had to really yell into her cell phone.

People in the store looked at us as if we were cranky wife and henpecked husband, and avoided the section of the store we were in.

When she yelled "less salt less salt" into the phone, it sounded like she was yelling "assault assault" and heads really started to turn. It was so embarrassing that I turned bright red and pushed the cart behind a display.

I later told her to send Grannie a letter next time.

Guns And Roses Iron Maiden Concert

First of all, I really didn't really want to go to this concert. Myself and my brother were drinking all day and we were poopeyed (at least I was). I still didn't want to go.

My idea was if I got pushed or shoved I wanted to retaliate. I am no fighter but I hate getting pushed or shoved.

We went to the concert. We had our coats full of beer and I had my binoculars (barnoculars) full of eight ounces of whiskey and eight ounces of Fine Old Canadian sherry.

As fate would have it, I met up with a fellow taekwondo student and we made friends quickly. Being a drunken fool, I confronted the guy with a playful attack. He put me on my ass pretty quick.

Two more attacks later I was still landing on my ass. The best man won.

Even though we were just playing around, the cops thought we were fighting. Off we went to the drunk tank.

Here we are in the drunk tank. I'm drunker than a fart. This guy has been kicked out of the concert because of me. He's pissed off and he is scary. He hits the Plexiglas and so do I. He kicks the Plexiglas and so do I. Eventually in my drunken state I hit the Plexiglas with my head trying to outdo him.

Oooh, I am now a tough guy. Anyways I got let out. I walked home and realized I forgot my hat. Off I went back to the detention center. I got my hat and walked back home.

I then realized I forgot my jacket. Kicking up a fuss I went back. I got my jacket. I walked back home and realized I forgot my barnoculars.

By then the guy behind the desk was getting quite p155ed off so I went home (before I got arrested). I eventually picked up my barnoculars a week later, after I completely sobered up.

I hope the concert was good.

KFC

I'll never forget the time Dad sent me to KFC to get a barrel of chicken. I mean that frigging thing was huge, and heavy.

I tripped and dropped it onto the Saint George Street sidewalk. I didn't know what to do, so I scraped up the gritty chicken and put it back into the barrel. I made it home and set it on the dining room table.

Everybody was eating it, except me. I didn't like chicken (especially on that day). I recall somebody making the comment that the chicken was real crunchy.

People chewed and crunched away until Dad found part of a cigarette butt on a piece of chicken. Finally he asked me what happened, and I told him I dropped the chicken on the sidewalk.

I thought he was going to yell (very loudly), but instead, gave me more money and sent me for more chicken telling me not to drop it this time.

This time I was very careful and got the chicken home safely.

Kraft Dinner

It was a nice day for pedaling, so off to Arnold's bread store I went. He had bread on sale, so I bought four loaves at 89 cents each.

The church bells were ringing at St Augustine's Church and I thought to myself, "What a glorious Sunday."

I figured I'd pedal to the bank and pay some money on my credit card and headed off. Coming back home I saw a sign at SDM saying Sunday Special Kraft Dinner three for a dollar.

"Whoopie!" I thought. I went in to buy a few boxes. I was dismayed to see eighty eight cents a box on the shelf.

I asked the cashier about the price and he told me eighty eight cents was the price, but three for a dollar on Sundays. Oh boy, today is Sunday so I bought nine boxes.

I thought, "This is even cheaper than Giant Tiger." I got home and saw that I paid seven dollars and ninety two cents.

"Holy #&*%" I said to myself. Then I realized it was only Saturday. I'm glad I didn't buy thirty boxes.

Story Update:

I pedaled back and embarrassedly explained my story about the church bells ringing and how I thought it was Sunday.

The girl mentioned that it was probably a wedding. She then gladly refunded my money and I told her I'd be back tomorrow. I then bought a box for eighty eight cents because I figured I'd be a good sport.

I thought I'd saved four dollars and ninety two cents by pedaling back, but in reality I still have to pedal back again tomorrow.

Mathematically, I pedaled halfway across town for two dollars and forty six cents. Oh well, I need my exercise.

Marilyn Monroe

I remember the time I took a private jet (air ambulance) from Moncton to Halifax. They loaded me onto the stretcher with a bit of difficulty as I was about 270 pounds at the time.

It was a nice flight. There were no delays and my luggage never got lost. All was going well until I had to get off the plane. I was a bit too heavy to maneuver the stretcher from the ground.

They tried and tried, but had no luck. Somebody had the idea for me to walk off the steps then carry the stretcher off.

This was a brilliant idea except for one flaw. As I was stepping onto the tarmac a big gust of wind blew my Johnny shirt up in the air like Marilyn Monroe.

It was quite embarrassing as there seemed to be a lot of people looking the airport window. I was glad to have brown hair as Gentlemen Prefer Blondes.

DANNY BURRIS

Mrs. Wuddle Drinking

Mrs. Wuddle hates drinking. She even hates sipping or guzzling.

One night we were at the Warehouse and I, believe it or not, was getting quite tipsy. She told me it was time for us to go. I told her I still had two beer left. She said to drink them and went to the bathroom.

Feeling a bit henpecked, I drank them both and ordered a couple more.

Not seeing the humour in the situation, she said, "We're leaving."

I told her I had two beer to go. She grabbed them and swigged them back with blinding speed.

I said, "What about my brother's beer?"

She drank it very fast and I figured "I'm not messing with that b*tch" and we left for two reasons.

One was because I was scared she might get rowdy, and the other was I couldn't really afford to buy her beer that fast.

My Chest Pain

I was working one Saturday night and my chest starting feeling sore. I figured it was the smokers trying to kill me, or a lung infection.

I slept fairly well that night, despite my tender chest. I got up Sunday morning and the chest was still sore. I spent the next 16 hours at work with the smokers trying to kill me all day. I cleaned out the hotdog machine 3 times that day, eating 10 hotdogs.

After work, I said to myself, "Self, this is enough. We gotta get this checked out."

Off to the hospital I drove, circling 'round and around looking for a parking spot. I finally found one about a block away and reluctantly put a quarter into the parking meter.

I told the person in the emergency room why I was there and sat down in the waiting room. My ass no sooner touched the chair when I was getting checked out. The doctor took my blood pressure. It was 231/213.

I almost had a heart attack when he told me I was having a heart attack. I thought, "Oh no, I have to work tomorrow night." I hated to miss a day of work and sometimes crawled in on 3 toes in the past.

I ended up in the hospital for 3 weeks. At least I didn't waste that quarter I put in the parking meter.

DANNY BURRIS

My Barbeque in the Park

It was a great day for a barbeque and I was going to enjoy my day off whether I liked it or not. It was going to be my last barbeque of the season and I was all excited about going to Fundy Park.

I didn't get very much sleep in the past two nights because I was so gung ho about going to the park. I finally got there and cracked open a liter bottle of Fine Old sherry. I drank the bottle and ate both steaks I had brought then got to feeling no pain.

I decided to take a nap so I set up the hammock between two trees. When I went to get into the hammock, one of the trees snapped and almost fell over. I called it a stupid piece of deadwood and gave it a kick. I didn't realize till then that a dead tree can fight back.

A piece of the tree top about a foot long and about six inches in diameter came crashing down on my head hurting like heck. I was cranky, so I put the still lit barbeque in the back of the pickup and away I went.

A few miles down the road I decided to go mountain climbing up this very steep slope. I got up about three quarters of the way as it started to get dark. I decided to go home.

I tripped coming down, adding to my already irritated level. Off I went. The new CD player was sounding great and so was the heater in the truck. I was getting comfortable, a little too comfortable.

I closed my eyes for a moment then heard a loud grinding noise. I opened my eyes to see fireworks right next to my window.

Man oh man they were pretty. I soon realized they weren't fireworks, but the side of my truck grinding away at the guardrail on the wrong side of the road.

I woke up pretty quick, just as my door started to come off. I swore to never fall asleep at the wheel again. Trust me, I swear, I swore. I hardly ever swear but I was very cranky by then.

I grabbed the door and held on to it as I drove the rest of the way home from Hillsborough to Moncton.

DANNY BURRIS

My Broken Foot

I once purchased a Honda 350 for $125.00. It had a bit of a wobble, so the guy I bought it from took it to a local back yard mechanic. It cost me $10.00 to get the wobble fixed.

The bike was looking pretty good considering I only had $135.00 tied up in it. I proceeded to drive it home. I got a couple of blocks down the road and noticed it needed gas, so I stopped to fill it up. I could not get the gas cap open. I tried and tried.

Finally I put down the kickstand and, straddling the bike, really came on to it with both hands, pounding and twisting it as hard as I could.

The bike moved a bit and fell off the kickstand, breaking my foot in two places. It cost me $14.00 to get taxis to and from the hospital.

Now I had $149.00 invested in the bike. I sold the bike for $150.00 making $1.00 profit, but ended up missing three weeks of work.

My Moped

I remember when my parents bought me a new moped. It was great fun to drive. I drove it everywhere.

I was saddened when it croaked on me about two days after I got it. I hoped it was still under warranty as I started pushing it from Miles Road towards Moncton to the repair shop.

I had the great idea of pedaling it, but soon realized the pedals were for looks and decided to start pushing again.

As I passed by Ed Holleran's garage, I had a great idea. Why not put gas in it? I was getting such great gas mileage I completely forgot to put gas in it.

It took less than a quarter worth of gas to fill it, then I was on my way again. I made a mental note to fill it up every couple of days from that point on.

Naval Base Dam

I remember my first trip back to the Naval Base Dam. We walked way out into the wilderness to see this thing. The thing looked like Niagara Falls at the time.

I was actually scared as we climbed the fifteen feet or so in the middle of winter.

My feet were starting to get cold, so we decided we needed to start a fire. There was an old outhouse that we remodeled into a nice bonfire. Mike Holmes couldn't have done a better job.

We survived the day and headed back to civilization.

New Driver's License

I used to work at Highfield Square in Moncton and walked to work and home to East Riverview every day. I bought a car, and was very happy the day I got my driver's license.

When I got off work I rushed home to celebrate. I was half way across the Gunningsville Bridge when I realized I forgot something.

I had to walk back to Highfield Square to get my car.

Nice Car

My truck had a flat tire in Moncton's Industrial Park. I started walking then noticed my buddy Mark's car in the parking lot where he worked.

I went in and he let me borrow his car. I noticed that he had fixed the body work. Then I noticed the new stereo. Nice, I thought to myself.

Then it was Holy Shit, I never noticed the sunroof before.

As I was leaving the parking lot I noticed Mark's car a few rows of traffic away. Holy Geeze, I was driving the wrong car.

Mark's Honda Accord was now a Honda Prelude. I discretely exchanged cars, got my tire fixed, and parked the other car in the wrong spot.

From what I heard there was a small bit of confusion when they both got off work.

Nice Little Kitty

I was pedaling home one night and noticed a cute little kitten coming out of the field near where I used to live. I stopped the bike and leaned down saying, "Here kitty kitty".

The kitten started coming towards me and I bent down to pick it up. It turned and lifted its tail and I realized it was no little kitty but a baby skunk.

I came on to the bike pedals as hard as I could, letting out a little chirp from the back tire as I took off before he peed.

Nofur

I came into the flea market one morning half asleep and partially hungover. I was eating my breakfast and heard a rustling noise coming from under one of my tables.

The noise stopped so I continued eating. Then it happened, a chihuahua peeked out its head. I went down to look at it.

Then what appeared to look like a big rat jumped out from under the table. I jumped up, and spilling my breakfast, started to run.

It was then Nofur came out and introduced himself with a "Meow". I knew he was a cat but had no fur, hence the name "Nofur". We have been friends ever since. Here's the little fellow's website if you ever want to meet him:

http://nofuratu.blogspot.ca/

Peanuts

I used to love to go to The Warehouse Pub. For anybody who never heard of The Warehouse Pub, they had barrels full of free peanuts. You drank your beer, ate your peanuts, and just tossed the shells onto the floor

On a busy night you could be walking around in ankle deep peanut shells.

It was closing time so I asked if I could take my cup full of peanuts home with me. I was walking along Main Street when a squad car pulled up beside me.

The officer asked me what I had in the cup.

I told him peanuts.

Thinking I was being a smartass he jumped out of the car, pinned me over the hood, and looked in the glass. When he saw the peanuts, did he ever look embarrassed.

After that I decided to have fun and stay on Main Street, waving at every squad car going by, with my cup of peanuts still in my hand.

DANNY BURRIS

Penny Picker

I have always picked up pennies when I found them.

One person I know from Snob Hill used to think that was so comical. He started dropping them on the floor at work so I'd pick them up just for laughs.

His friends thought it was funny and, they too, started dropping them on the floor. They started tossing pennies under tables and in corners. They even started opening up the front door and throwing pennies at the back of my head when I was cleaning up at night.

After about a year and a half I had accumulated a vast wealth of almost $40.00. The guy who started throwing the pennies at me needed to borrow money one time, so I loaned him $30.00 in pennies charging him $3.00 extra for interest.

When he paid me back I laughed all the way to the beer store.

Pool Table

Once I was helping somebody move three pool tables from Memramcook to Moncton.

A coin operated pool table weighs 850 pounds with the slate being the heaviest part at 500 pounds. We took the pool tables apart and loaded them into the cube van.

All was going well until we got to Dieppe. It was then that an old man with a hat (the worst drivers in the world are old men with hats, just ask anybody who drives for a living) pulled out in front of us almost causing an accident. One of the pool tables started moving and crashed through the little door ending up in the cab of the truck.

I'll never forget the truck driver's reaction. His hat was bouncing up and down on his head as he yelled, "You old bat. I'll bat you in the side of the head you old bat."

Some of us remember that quote and practically piss ourselves laughing at it over 32 years later.

Smoking at the Store

Every day we used to stop by Ned's store on the way to school and hang out there. The bigger kids used to smoke in the store thinking they were tough.

One day one came up to me and said, "Here, hold my smoke for a minute."

I never smoked in my life and nervously held his cigarette for him. Another kid got me to do the same thing. Soon I was holding four lit cigarettes, two in each hand. I didn't know what was going on.

I soon found out when one of the teachers walked into the store. No pun is intended when I say I was a smoke screen for the other kids.

The teacher took one look at me, shook her head, and left the store. I don't think she really believed I smoked that much especially at ten or eleven years old.

SS Houdini

Myself and the Skipper went to what we used to call The Winding River for a boating excursion. We decided to blow up the boat early in the morning then bring it later in the day. It was a brilliant idea and would have saved us about five minutes of time where we could better use it by drinking a couple of beer.

We made it to the stream and noticed the boat was missing. We headed back and found the boat sitting in the middle of the road about two miles back.

How it got out of the truck with the cover door closed we couldn't figure it out. We loaded the "SS Houdini" back into the truck and put bungie cords on the door.

We were behind schedule and had to drink our beer faster.

One of us tripped into the water while getting into the boat. It has never been proven which one it was.

DANNY BURRIS

Stand Up

I remember when I was in a wheelchair. The nurses would have to push me to the bathroom then I'd have to use the guide rails to sit down on the terlit and do my business, sitting down to pee.

One night I decided to stand up to pee. I waited for the nurse to close the door, then tried to stand up and do my business.

All was going well until my pants fell down. Try and try as I might, I could not get down to pull them up.

After a while the nurse decided to check me and caught me with my bare arse with my pants around my feet. I was quite em bare assed over the whole thing.

Stuck In The Bar

I was working one Sunday with a snow storm going on outside. My boss told me to close up for 3 pm.

People just started coming in like crazy after he said that. I couldn't turn that much business away.

At around 7 pm I finally got the place cleared out and was ready to walk home.

John, the bar manager, showed up and we each had a beer. Soon a couple of good customers knocked on the bar door and I let them in. We inhaled many a brew.

One customer pointed out that Miller Highlife was on sale for $1.25 a can and we cleared out the fridge of that product.

We were getting poopeyed by then and somebody had the idea to pile the cans up to the ceiling in the middle of the bar. I did not mention my name for this idea.

At about 3 am we were all pretty full and decided to call it a night. I was glad I worked the following night shift because I guess the poop really hit the fan the next day.

The other 3 guys really got blasted from head office.

The Bicycle Rack

I've been told I'm sometimes not the sharpest pencil in the box. I looked at Moncton's busses for about two weeks trying to figure how they get the wheelchairs to stay on the front of them.

Then one day I watched some stupid ass try to fit his bike on it. He was determined to get the bike to fit.

By George, he was right. It was made for a bike, not a wheelchair.

It was too windy to sit up there with a wheelchair anyway.

The Camera

I remember a few years back when I had to get some medical test done. It involved swallowing a PillCam and having it go through your system taking about 10,000 pictures along the way, and coming out a few days later.

The pictures were saved through a wireless system.

I asked about the camera and was told they flushed it away when it came out.

I decided to intercept it and clean it up before showing people it at the flea market. Every day I looked for the camera but had no luck finding it.

Finally about a week later I knew it was coming. I sat on the terlit and waited then waited some more. As luck would have it I fell asleep on the terlit.

I was woken up by a nurse who helped me up as she flushed the terlit. I think I could see my camera going down the drain. What a waste of time watching my poop for a week.

Oh well, at least I still have the case the pill came in.

DANNY BURRIS

The Chemistry Set

Once I got a chemistry set for Christmas. I was quite excited about it and could hardly wait to try it out.

A couple of days later I took it out to the back porch and decided to become a scientist. I filled the alcohol burner with lighter fluid and proceeded to experiment away.

I lit the burner and BOOM, it blew up, setting the porch on fire.

I hollered, "Mom, mom, bring me some water," and she came out with a glass of water. Was she ever surprised.

She brought out a lot more water and we put out the fire. Nobody in our family has gotten a chemistry set ever since then.

The Ferris Wheel

Once upon a time a few years back I was on a Ferris wheel enjoying the ride. It stopped with me on the top.

The wind started up and the seat started rocking back and forth. It kept going faster and faster. I closed my eyes in fear.

When I reopened my eyes I was standing at the edge of my bed swaying back and forth before taking a nose dive and landing flat on my face on the floor.

I was grateful it was only a dream, but it still ended up hurting like heck.

The Flock

My pal John and I went on a pink flamingo safari in Riverview once upon a time. Over a 6 or 7 day period we had rounded up almost all the pink flamingos in town.

He did most of the capturing while I, being scared of getting caught, mostly sat in and guarded the getaway car.

A friend of mine had just built a new house and hated pink flamingos, so guess what happened. One night we planted the pink flamingos all over his front lawn.

There must have been about a hundred of the little buggers. You should have seen the look on the guy's face when he looked out the front door. I almost fell off my motorbike laughing when I saw him and waved.

Rumour has it he was out harvesting pink flamingos with a golf club after a few minutes.

The Hot Rod

If you remember, back in the early 80s skate boards started to gain popularity. They were short compared to today's models.

Although none of us did any tricks with them, they were fun to ride. We would start at the top of Runnymead Street in Riverview (about 1/10 mile) and ride down them over and over.

Of course, being an unofficial part-time genius, I had to create what I called The Hot Rod. This was an engineering marvel.

I took an ashtray stand and placed a bicycle seat on it. It was solid looking and appeared to be quite well built.

I hopped on it at the top of the hill and went down about a third of the way with no problem until the thing turned. It was then I decided it needed a steering wheel.

Rolling down the hill backwards, I also discovered I should have installed breaks. I went arse over tea kettle into the ditch.

I eventually got up from the ditch and brought The Hot Rod back home.

Dad could smoke again and my sister could ride her bike. I gave up on the dream of building hot rods.

The Long Haul

When I was in the wheelchair, I was supposed to roll around the nurse station to get exercise.

There was one day when it was so hard to get there that I almost gave up. The wheelchair was just too hard for me to move.

Still, I persevered and tried my best to get to the hospital door.

It was then that I realized that somehow my wheelchair had hooked on the bed and it was being pulled behind me.

I was so tired I didn't even bother trying to reverse the bed back the six inches to its rightful stop.

The Massage

Once myself and a friend of mine were eating pizza and drinking beer.

He asked me if I ever visited the local massage parlour. I told him no. He offered to pay, so off we went.

We got there and I paid the $45.00 he gave me. Guess what? My little soldier wouldn't stand up.

Maybe it was the fact that they got raided a week before and I was scared of being on the news in front of my grandmother.

I walked away wasting my friend's $45.00.

Later I got to doing some thinking. What if the masseuse thought I was gay? I am a straight arrow.

The next week I popped a few vitamins and parked my car at Highfield Square. I started to jog to the place I had failed before.

I saw my best friend's grannie sitting on a lawn chair across the street from my destination. I waved and jogged on by.

A few blocks later she was still there. I jogged by again. The third time I jogged by she was in the house, so I entered my destination.

I was pumped. I paid the $45.00 and hoped for the best.

I got a different girl so I proved nothing. I was so pumped that I expired my time.

The girl told me that she gave me 15 minutes extra and she had other people waiting. She said I would have to finish the job myself.

I jogged back to the car $45.00 poorer and proving to a different girl that I wasn't gay.

The Parking Lot

One December day I sat on my bed and was poked in the ass by a bed spring.

I got some type of infection and after a couple of days I drove my truck to the hospital to get checked out.

It was after midnight and the gate to the parking lot was up because nobody was working. I drove in. I ended up spending 3 days in the hospital.

When I went to pay for my parking I had no ticket, so the guy at the gate wanted to charge me for 4 days. All I had was $20.00 and 4 days would cost me $22.00.

Off to catch the bus I went. I went to Riverview where I picked up my paycheck then got a ride to the bank. I went home for a nap and woke up after 11pm.

It was New Years Eve, so I walked to my parents' house to wish them a Happy New Year, then it was off to pick up my truck. I got back, and wonder of wonders, the gate was open.

I drove up to it and asked at the empty booth, "How much do I owe?" I listened carefully and heard nothing so nothing is what I paid and away I went.

Wahoooooo..........I now had beer money for my next day off.

The Pool Party

It was a nice day and the boss decided to have a pool party. As people were getting there they all got chucked into the pool.

I was having fun and was getting good exercise. All was going well until we got into a semi drunken state and went to throw one guy in. If I recall correctly he was hard to catch and went sailing over the pool to the other side.

Sorry Stumpy.

Oh, and thanks for the beer.

The Purse

I have a bad case of Purso-phobia. I cannot hold a purse.

My better half can't seem to understand if she asks me and I refuse to hold her purse for even one second.

My most embarrassing moment was a triple bad moment. I was getting off the #14 Riverview bus one day and noticed a lady had left her purse on the seat. I grabbed the purse and ran after her down the sidewalk in front of Highfield Square.

All the people were staring. If that wasn't bad enough when I caught up with her and tapped her on the shoulder she was startled and turned letting out a yell.

I told her about her purse and she told me it wasn't hers. I decided to give it to the bus driver, and wheezing loudly from running my mini marathon, proceeded to walk back to the bus with the purse under my arm.

Of course it had to be at 5pm in front of seemingly everybody from Moncton. I gave the purse to the bus driver and started walking home swearing "Never Again".

The Salad Incident

One night I was pedaling my bike and stopped at the Strikes and Spares Bar, which used to be on Pine Glenn Road in Riverview, for a few brew.

The bartender cashed my pay check and I bought a couple hundred dollars' worth of quarters, figuring the quarters would last longer than paper money would.

I put the quarters in the carrier bag on my bike and proceeded to get poopeyed. After a while the bartender called for a taxi to take me home.

I arrived home in Moncton and asked the taxi driver how much I owed, and he told me the bartender already paid. I thought that was awfully good of her and decided to go buy her dinner.

Well, off I went. I stopped at the Pizza Delight, which used to be at the end of the causeway, and bought us each a Caesar salad and started pedaling across the causeway.

I got racing with a Camaro. He got stuck behind an old Datsun or something and I passed him on the inside laughing away.

It was then I realized we were at the floodgates and I was heading for a curb. Over the handlebars I went with the salad and quarters flying everywhere.

The Caesar salad was now a tossed salad.

I loaded up the bike and continued on my way. I got back to the bar and after I got my wounds attended to, I offered the bartender a salad.

She politely declined so I ate them both.

The next day I pedaled past where I'd had my accident and picked up over $70.00 worth of loose quarters.

DANNY BURRIS

The Shortcut

Once I took a shortcut from Turtle Creek Road to Trites Road along the power lines on my dirt bike.

There was a lot of mud on the way, and many puddles. Needless to say I got dirty.

At one point, I stopped to take a leak and the bike sank into the mud with just a mirror sticking out. At the end of my trip I was covered with mud and had torn the bottoms off both of my sneakers.

Off to Woolco in Champlain Place I went. I asked the girl at the cashier where the footwear section was, then hiked through the store leaving muddy footprints as I went.

After paying for them, I put the new sneakers on and put the old ones in the bag.

Off for home I went, muddy, sore, and tired.

The Snowstorm

I went to work one night during a snow storm, only to find the place closed up. My truck got stuck in the parking lot and I was ticked off.

My buddy drove by and we pushed the truck, but had no results.

I hopped in his car and it was off to his place to sip beverages and shoot pool. His licker was good and we drank a couple of bottles.

Soon all the licker was gone and we had to get out. My buddy asked his wife if it was ok to give me a drive home. She asked where I lived and he told her I lived in Sussex.

Wahoo, we were out of the house. We loaded his husky dog into the car and listened to Millie Vanillie of all things as we drove to Moncton.

We stopped by my place and grabbed a quart of vodka.

The car got stuck in the middle of Mountain Road, so we drank the vodka while the dog ran up and down the street.

Soon we ended up at the Shipyard. Guess who was playing.........Ray Lyell And "The Storm". It was an excellent show.

I got very, very shitfaced but somehow managed to dig my way home through the snow.

The Winter Carnival

Going to NBCC was a lot of fun. I got to go to lots of parties and meet a lot of people. I really liked Winter Carnival Week.

Our tug of war team took second place.

On the final day we had the pie eating contest and the chug a lug contest. I took first place gobbling down my chocolate cream pie and looked at my closest competitor. She had about half of her pie eaten, so I jumped over and ate the other half.

After a break it was off to The Little Rock for the chug a lug contest where I got to proudly be our anchorman.

For those who don't know how a chugging contest goes, there are four members on a team. Here's how our contest went:

The first member chugs a draft.
The second member chugs a draft.
The third member chugs a draft.
The anchorman chugs two drafts.
The third member chugs a draft.
The second member chugs a draft.
The first member chugs a draft.

We had a couple of practice rounds and all was well. Our teacher stopped by and paid for another round and all was better.

It was competition time. We tied the other team and had to do another round. We played another round and ended up taking second place.

We were shaking hands and I started to feel sick. My meal of a pie and a half and ten drafts was not going to stay down.

The Little Rock had wall to wall people. Nobody would get out of the way. I climbed up on the long row of tables and ran down the center towards the bathroom, knocking over a couple of glasses along the way.

I finally made it to the bathroom and met another competitor coming out. He insisted on shaking my hand. He told me his name but I introduced myself as RALLLLLPH.

I don't think he enjoyed my meal anywhere near as much as I originally did.

Trip to Newfoundland

The night before my trip to Newfoundland I got poopeyed and gave myself a haircut (shaved my head).

The next day I woke up and we were off to Newfoundland. It was a stormy day in Moncton, and my head was freezing, but at least I was out of bed. We were off on our adventure.

The boat ride to Newfoundland was very rough but the more I drank the better I stood up.

We arrived in Newfoundland early next morning. Wahoooo, we were off to Trout River.

You should see all the Newfies in Newfoundland. There's almost as many there as in Toronto.

From what I figure in Trout River it is bad manners to knock on a person's door. You have to just walk in.

There are so many nice people in Trout River, just like the rest of Newfoundland.

The highlight of my Trout River trip was when we rode Buddy's snowmobile down Main Street in a snowstorm to go to the beer store. It was the best vacation I ever took.

A Trip to the Zoo

I remember I was enjoying a trip to the zoo. I was feeding the ducks and swans and was having a grand old time.

I fed some deer and they seemed to like my cooking. I didn't tell them it came from a vending machine.

I wondered around and came to the petting zoo. That was pretty nice.

Finally I got to the monkey cage. I tossed one little fellow a banana. He ate it, then I felt it raining.

Mrs. W. told me to look up and the little bugger was peeing on me. I thought this was rather rude of him and we exchanged some very explicit language.

I tried to biff him in the head with another banana, but he was too fast and too high up in the tree.

Walk With Your Walker

After I got out of my wheelchair I had to start using a walker. Somehow I was always leaning on it too hard and the wheels were always wobbly and ready to fall off.

I decided to walk around without it. As I walked past the nurse's station, I was intercepted by a nurse who told me not to walk without the walker.

If you know me, you know I always listen to authority figures and so I went to get my walker. I folded up my walker then placed it under my arm and proceeded to walk around the nurse's station again.

I told her, "See, I have my walker."

The nurse was not impressed, and I'm glad she didn't throw something at me.

I quickly hobbled back to my room and hid there until the next morning.

At least I wasn't walking without my walker.

About the Author

I'm a retired old geezer who had to leave the workplace due to medical reasons. Rather than sit and look out the window all day and get old, I started going to the flea market. I really don't make any money but find it a very rewarding experience. It helps me fill the void of being unemployed by creating the illusion that I have a job.

I get to hang out with a lot of great people. Sometimes I go home after a weekend with a few dollars in my pocket and drop it into the can at the soup kitchen (while enjoying a few great meals). It's a good feeling to know that, even though I live below the poverty level, I can still enjoy the luxury of being able to give to charity from time to time.

Many thanks go to Donna Carrick for all she has done for in helping me with this book. Her knowledge and patience is very much appreciated.

IT'S A WUDDLEFUL LIFE

DANNY BURRIS